The
Perfect
Conference

The Perfect Conference

ALL YOU NEED
TO GET IT RIGHT
FIRST TIME

IAIN MAITLAND

ARROW
BUSINESS BOOKS

Published by Arrow Books in 1994

1 3 5 7 9 10 8 6 4 2

First published by
Arrow Books Limited
20 Vauxhall Bridge Road, London SW1V 2SA

Random House Australia (Pty) Limited
20 Alfred Street, Milsons Point, Sydney
New South Wales 2061, Australia

Random House New Zealand Limited
18 Poland Road, Glenfield
Auckland 10, New Zealand

Random House South Africa (Pty) Limited
PO Box 337, Bergvlei, South Africa

Random House UK Limited Reg. No. 954009

ISBN 0-09-937911-2

Set in Bembo by
SX Composing Ltd, Rayleigh, Essex
Printed and bound in Great Britain by
Cox and Wyman Ltd, Reading, Berks

British Library Cataloguing in Publication Data
A catalogue record for this book is available from
the British Library

For Tracey, Michael and Sophie

ACKNOWLEDGEMENTS

Thanks are due to the following individuals and organizations who provided me with helpful information during the compilation of this text:

Terry Billingham, Connect

John Charlton, Conferences and Exhibitions Diary

Karen Charter, Association of Conference Executives

Heather Chester, The Meetings Industry Association

Anne Collins, Holiday Inn Worldwide

Robert Enefa, The Conference People

Susie Helme, Conference and Exhibition Fact Finder

Patricia Moore, British Tourist Authority

Jean Neville, Benn Business Information Services Limited

Tony Rogers, British Association of Conference Towns

ABOUT THE AUTHOR

Iain Maitland is a freelance author and journalist. He has written over 20 books for organizations such as the Institute of Management, the *Daily Telegraph*, Barclays Bank and the Institute of Personnel Development. His articles have been published in many newspapers and magazines including the *Daily Express, Management Week, Retail Week*, and *Personnel Today*.

You can contact Iain Maitland by writing to him care of his agents – Chelsey Fox and Charlotte Howard of the Fox and Howard Literary Agency, 4 Bramerton Street, Chelsea, London SW3 5JX; Tel: 071 352 0561; Fax: 071 352 8691.

CONTENTS

INTRODUCTION

The Perfect Conference is written for you – the panic-stricken executive who has been given the dubious responsibility for setting up such an event for your company. More than likely, you are expected to do this in addition to your usual workload *and* to make a huge success of it – despite the fact that you have never arranged one before! In four easy stages, this book shows you how to succeed.

Stage One: Organizing a Conference is divided into three chapters. *Making Plans* examines different types of conferences, recognizing your goals and establishing your budget. *Drafting a Programme* details picking a theme, sketching out contents and preparing a schedule. *Selecting the Venue* encompasses analysing your requirements, looking at locations, studying venues and paying a visit to them.

Stage Two: Promoting a Conference is an extremely important ingredient which needs to be contemplated carefully. *Attracting Participants* sets out how to commission speakers, invite delegates and publicize the event to the outside world. *Bringing in Outsiders* moves on to investigate using specialists, negotiating with suppliers and referring to trade bodies in the conference industry.

Stage Three: Running a Conference focuses on the event itself. *Working with Speakers* covers speaking in public, staging rehearsals and implementing changes. *Handling Equipment* discusses including visual and audio-visual aids in the programme, and how to make the most of any equipment used. *Looking after Participants* spans taking care of delegates, managing miscellaneous matters and entertaining everyone – speakers, delegates *and* partners.

The fourth and final stage, **Evaluating a Conference**, is often ill considered by organizers although it is just as significant as the other stages. *Reviewing the Event* suggests that you look back, considering your organizational activities, thinking about promotional techniques and assessing your tactics at the conference. *Following Through* advises you to turn to the future, writing a report, improving yourself and planning ahead for next time. *Further Reading* and *Useful Addresses* sections complete the book.

The clear and concise comments, easy to read format and use of checklists at appropriate intervals, will provide you with all the information you need to organize, promote, run and evaluate a conference. Staging a successful event first time around *can* be done and with the help of this handy and compact guide, you can hold that perfect conference – and prove everybody wrong!

Iain Maitland

ORGANIZING A CONFERENCE

1. MAKING PLANS

Identifying your conference

Recognizing your goals

Establishing your budget

2. DRAFTING A PROGRAMME

Picking a theme

Sketching out contents

Preparing a schedule

3. SELECTING THE VENUE

Analyzing your requirements

Looking at locations

Studying venues

Paying a visit

1
MAKING PLANS

Organizing the perfect conference requires careful thought and planning. When making plans, you should identify the type of conference you are going to run, recognize your goals and establish your budget. Once these key, preliminary tasks have been completed, you can move on to draft a programme and select the venue for your winning conference.

IDENTIFYING YOUR CONFERENCE

Every conference is unique, with its own individual blend of speakers, delegates, contents and so on. Nonetheless, conferences can be grouped together under various headings – and it is sensible to be aware of which group your conference is in. Not surprisingly, the type of conference being staged will have a huge influence on the ways in which you subsequently organize, promote, run and evaluate that conference. Here are some typical types:

Sales
These may be set up for your own sales team and/or intermediaries, to review sales targets and results to date and to motivate people to work harder and better in the future.

Incentive
A variation of sales conferences, these are often held in unusual or exotic locations, and for a select number of successful salespeople only – thus acting as an incentive for *all* of the salesforce to achieve more, so that they can attend next time!

Promotional
Here, new or revised products or services may be launched or publicized to your sales team, independent

sellers or prospective buyers. The aim is to inform them about the goods and to persuade them to promote or buy the items, as appropriate.

Press
Similar to promotional conferences, these are staged to put across information to media representatives, with a view to obtaining publicity for your firm, products and services via newspapers, magazines, and so forth.

Trade
At these conferences, members of a professional or trade body and associated individuals meet to discuss past, present and future market trends, trade actions and responses.

Training
Although more often built into sales or trade conferences, separate events are sometimes staged in order to train staff, intermediaries or other, related people in various aspects of selling, trade or associated activities.

Other
In all probability, you will feel that your conference does not fit perfectly into any of these particular groupings, and that it should be in an 'other' category of its own. No matter – the fact that you focused on your conference and thought carefully about it before doing anything else is of greater importance.

RECOGNIZING YOUR GOALS
Your reasons for organizing this conference must be clear in your mind – after all, if you do not know where you are going, you are highly unlikely to arrive at the right place! Possibly the most efficient way of recognizing your goals quickly and easily is to ask yourself numerous 'who, what, when, where, why, how?' questions, and then answer them. Consider these, in particular:

Who?
Think about who you want to attend your conference, both in terms of speakers and delegates. Will it be an in-house affair, with the managing and sales directors speaking, and salespeople listening? Alternatively, do you wish to bring in speakers and delegates from outside? Are participants known or unknown?

What?
What do you want your speakers to put across – an informative message, or possibly an inspirational one? What do you want from the delegates – sales orders, perhaps, or free publicity?

When?
Contemplate when you wish to stage the conference, and for how long. For example, it may be wise to hold a trade conference during a trading lull, as few members will want to attend during their busiest periods. As a general rule – but remember rules exist to be broken – keep a conference short and to the point, to maintain interest and limit costs.

Where?
Whereabouts would you like to run a conference – on your premises, in a hotel or purpose-built conference centre, at a college or university, on a ship, or elsewhere? More importantly, where would the participants want it to be staged – somewhere accessible and pleasant?

Why?
Step back and consider why you are planning a conference – to motivate your salespeople? To reach a trade agreement? Is it really necessary? Bear in mind that a conference can be a time-consuming and expensive affair. Could you achieve your goals in another, easier manner? Possibly, a sales report, a promotional brochure or a press release would be just as successful.

How?

If – and it may be a big 'if' – you think a conference is worthwhile, how should it be conducted? A speaker talking to delegates *en masse*? Several speakers leading various, smaller sessions? Hard work, and no play? Some fun and games too, perhaps? A social programme for partners?

Hopefully, your tentative answers to these questions will provide you with a loose and flexible framework to work within and towards. Of course, there is much to do in each of these areas as you proceed, but at least you now have a better understanding of what you want and where you wish to go.

ESTABLISHING A BUDGET

Each conference differs in some way or another from every other one, and will thus have its own particular budget. Given the potential differences, it is hard to calculate a specific budget in advance, especially first time around. Nevertheless, an approximate budget should be set so that those involved in organizing, promoting, running and evaluating the conference know what can be spent, and in which areas. Take each step in turn, as follows:

Listing Costs

To begin with, it is a good idea to draw up a lengthy list of all of the prospective costs you can possibly think of. This is not a simple task, and you may find it easier to do if you jot down your thoughts under various sub-headings such as 'the venue', 'the speakers', 'the delegates', 'publicity' and so on, as in Figure 1.1.

The Essentials

You need to identify those costs which are absolutely essential in your situation. Obviously, these essentials must vary from one conference to another. For

Figure 1.1. Prospective Costs

- The Venue — basic hire
  - equipment hire
  - other facilities
  - other services
- Overnight Accommodation — basic hire
  - equipment hire
  - other facilities
  - other services
- The Speakers — location costs
  - invitations
  - fees
  - travel and accommodation
  - miscellaneous expenses
- The Delegates — location costs
  - invitations
  - travel and accommodation
  - miscellaneous extras
- Publicity — press releases; stationery, postage etc
  - directory entries
  - general advertising; trade magazines etc
  - other promotional activities
- Outsiders — specialists' fees; professional conference organizers etc
  - equipment purchase or hire
  - other services
  - trade association membership
- The Event — pre-conference documents; timetable, map etc
  - rehearsals
  - transport of equipment
  - technicians' fees
  - conference packs; revised timetable, product data etc
  - badges
  - registration desks, and staff
  - display material; banners, signs etc
  - security
  - safety
  - insurance; cancellation etc
  - general assistance; dogsbodies etc
  - catering; breaks, lunches, dinners etc
  - entertainment; disco, cabaret etc
  - other extras
- The Review — report of the event
  - books, magazines
  - training courses
- Other Costs — your time; time is money etc
  - colleagues' time
  - employees' time
  - value added tax
  - allowance for inflation; between now and then
  - allowance for mistakes; between now and then
- Total Costs — to be calculated

example, hiring a venue is an essential cost if you have to stage the conference midway between your firm and participants who are based some distance away, but is not applicable if you hold that conference at your head office. Insurance (in case your conference has to be cancelled, for example) is another essential cost.

The Desirables

Next, you should highlight those costs which would be desirable in your circumstances, and these might include payments for various on-site leisure facilities for participants, membership fees for trade bodies and miscellaneous minor gifts for delegates such as pens, pencils, bookmarks and the like. The remaining costs on your initial list can then be deleted.

The Final Figure

It is wise to try to work out minimum and maximum figures for each 'essential' and 'desirable'. Although this is not easy, it needs to be done, and at an early stage. Some costs can probably be estimated by you, drawing on your own knowledge and experience. Others might be anticipated by your colleagues and business contacts. Alternatively, various trade associations exist in the conference industry which can give advice. See *Useful Addresses*, page 79. However you do it, some form of budget needs to be pieced together.

The Cashflow Forecast

This is often overlooked. It is extremely useful to compile a cashflow forecast for the event, showing month-by-month when monies will be made available to you and when they will have to be paid out. You do need to make sure in advance that finance will always be there when it is required, rather than finding out at the last moment whether it is or not.

CHECKLIST FOR SUCCESS – ONE

- Have you identified your conference?

- Is it a sales, incentive, promotional, press, trade or training conference, or perhaps another type?

- Have your recognized your goals? Who, what, when, where, why and how?

- Have you established your budget?

- Did you list costs, the essentials and desirables, and then reach a final, flexible figure?

- Have you drafted a cashflow forecast too?

2

DRAFTING A PROGRAMME

With your initial preparatory work having been carried out, you can start to think about drafting a programme for your conference. Typically, this will involve picking a theme, sketching out contents and preparing a schedule – all very important ingredients in the successful preparation of a perfect conference.

PICKING A THEME

Many conferences have a theme, ranging from such matter-of-fact ones as 'Crop Protection' and 'Marine Exhaust Emissions' through to the rather more abstract 'Beyond the Millenium', 'Making it Happen' and the like. If the idea of having an overall theme appeals to you, it is essential to be aware of some of the key advantages and disadvantages before picking the right one for you.

Advantages

A theme can provide a backbone for your conference – referred to in invitations to speakers and delegates to create interest, repeated in publicity activities to attract attention, used as a common thread in speeches, set design and layout, supporting material and so on. If appropriate, it will help to put over your main message and build a solid, lasting impression of the conference and what it was about.

Disadvantages

Nevertheless, having an over-riding theme can cause problems. Often, an organizer has a theme because he or she feels there ought to be one, and a dramatic and memorable one at that – even though it may be unnecessary or have little to do with the actual contents of the event. It is easy to be too clever, which can be confusing. If a theme is relevant *and* understood, it is tempting to become too dependent on it, trying to maintain it throughout, even when it is less relevant or difficult to do so.

The Right Theme

Should you believe that a theme may be worthwhile in your situation, then be sure to pick one which sums up what you are trying to put across, so you can use that theme up to, during and beyond the event. Think about what will appeal to and attract your audience – in general, choose a specific, easy to understand theme such as 'Increasing Your Sales' or 'Improving The Environment' rather than vague and confusing ones such as 'Winning' or 'Getting it Right'.

SKETCHING OUT CONTENTS

Having thought carefully about the type of conference you are organizing, you should already have some ideas of what you want to include in that conference. For example, a sales conference divides itself up almost automatically into separate times for presenting sales figures, praising and rewarding successful sellers, discussing targets and so on. A promotional conference for a new product lends itself naturally to a presentation of the item, a general discussion, a period of testing the goods, a question and answer session, and so forth. When building up your framework of ideas, you should bear the following points in mind. Contents should be:

Relevant

At all times, know and concentrate on what you are trying to put over, whether detailed statistics about regional sales, technical data concerning a revamped product, or advice on completing various tasks and duties. Be conscious of your audience, and the best way in which they will absorb that message, perhaps via a straightforward speech, presentation or demonstration. Recognize your aims and what will help you to achieve them.

Interesting

Your conference needs to be interesting, if delegates are going to come along, listen, participate and react as you want them to do. There are many ways of maintaining interest, one of which is to incorporate opportunities for everyone to take part in the event, through discussions, question and answer sessions and so forth. Later on, when you have commissioned speakers, invited delegates and are close to finalizing contents, you can give additional thought to how speakers will address the audience, use visual and audio-visual aids and look after participants in order to keep them interested throughout the event.

Balanced

It is important that you strike a balance between business and pleasure – an endless succession of speeches, facts and figures and so on will meet with limited success. People can only take in so much information and after that will become bored and disgruntled. Break up the conference with reasonable coffee, lunch and tea breaks, and other opportunities to relax and unwind. If relevant, incorporate a social programme for delegates and their partners, perhaps with a visit to a nearby restaurant, theatre and/or leisure complex, as appropriate.

Brief

There is no ideal length for a conference, simply because every one of them is different from the rest – some may last a few hours, others several days. Obviously, much depends on what and how much you are trying to put across, and how quickly you wish to do it. Your conference should be sufficiently long to put over your message successfully, but short enough to retain concentration and minimize costs. Do not allow too much time for relaxing!

Flexible

Your contents should be flexible enough to be adjusted as you go along, to jiggle the order to make the best use of speakers, or add on sessions at the request of delegates, and so forth. At this stage, you should have a skeleton framework to be developed, amended and finalized closer to the event. An example of typical contents – so far as they exist – for a two–day sales conference is given in Figure 2.1.

PREPARING A SCHEDULE

It takes time to organize a conference – certainly longer than a few weeks or even a couple of months. Arguably, a small conference with perhaps 30 or so participants will take about three months to arrange properly, a larger one as long as a year or more. Do not attempt to rush it though – it will probably be unsuccessful, and you will be blamed! Set out a schedule, which may be similar to the one below in terms of order and content, although you will need to fill in the details and shorten or lengthen the time scale to suit your own circumstances.

Month 6

- Take the decision to stage a conference
- Appoint a conference organizer
- Identify the type of conference to be held
- Recognize goals
- Establish a budget
- Pick a theme
- Sketch out contents
- Prepare a schedule

Month 5

- Analyse location and venue requirements
- Look at locations
- Study possible venues

Figure 2.1. A Provisional Programme

- **Day One** – arrive at lunchtime (remember, delegates may be coming some distance so do not start too early)

  – lunch (not too heavy though, you want them to concentrate in the afternoon)

  – session one; introductory speeches by the managing and sales directors
  analysis of sales figures by type, region etc presented by the sales director

  – break for refreshments (and to visit the loo!)

  – session two; further analysis of sales figures, perhaps with handouts
  questions and answers from and to delegates chaired by the sales director

  – break to unwind at the hotel (or the bar!)

  – evening meal at the hotel; presentations to sales staff by the managing director

  – visit to the theatre (do book well in advance – and get good seats!)

- **Day Two** – breakfast (not too heavy – you still want their attention!)

  – session three; outline of company policy for the forthcoming year presented by the managing director
  questions and answers from and to delegates

  – break for refreshments (and a chance to 'compare notes')

  – session four; outline of sales policy and targets for the forthcoming year presented by the sales director
  general discussion with the delegates

  – lunch (as heavy as you like!); closing speeches by the managing and sales directors, thanks and congratulations

  – time to depart (perhaps for the long journey home!)

- Visit shortlisted venues and accommodation
- Make provisional bookings for venue, accommodation, facilities and services

Month 4

- Commission speakers
- Invite delegates
- Amend conference contents
- Publicize the event
- Check the budget and cash flow are on target
- Firm up provisional bookings
- Liaise with venue, as appropriate

Month 3

- Bring in specialists, if relevant
- Negotiate with suppliers of equipment, catering, entertainment and other facilities
- Make bookings for facilities and services, as required
- Arrange insurance cover
- Refer to trade associations, if necessary
- Conduct more publicity
- Liaise with venue, speakers and delegates, as relevant

Month 2

- Finalize details with the venue
- Confirm contents with speakers
- Check delegates' travel, accommodation and attendance arrangements
- Finalize suppliers' details and arrangements
- Carry out last-minute publicity
- Double-check the budget and cash flow are on course

Month 1

- Visit venue to see all is in order
- Rehearse contents with speakers

- Get the delegates there
- Make sure equipment is working well
- Ready to go?

Obviously, this particular schedule will differ from every other one. Some organizers will say it is too short or long a time, others too brief or detailed, and a proportion will complain about its exact order. The key point is that *you* set a timetable which allows *you* plenty of time to do everything *you* need to do, and in an order of *your* choice.

CHECKLIST FOR SUCCESS – TWO

- Have you thought about picking a theme?

- Did you weigh up the advantages and disadvantages before making a choice?

- Have you sketched out the likely contents of your conference?

- Are they relevant, balanced, brief and flexible?

- Have you prepared a schedule? Perhaps over six, twelve or even eighteen months?

3

SELECTING THE VENUE

The significance of a suitable venue must not be under-estimated – it can make or break the success of your conference. To make your choice, you should analyse your requirements, look at locations, study venues and pay a visit to shortlisted ones. Only then will you be able to reach the right decision in your circumstances.

ANALYSING YOUR REQUIREMENTS

Evidently, each conference is distinct, with its own particular mix of features distinguishing it from other ones. Therefore, conference organizers all have different needs when selecting a venue – which may account for the diversity of venues available nowadays from hotels through universities to ships! Consider these points before compiling your own individual set of requirements:

The Conference

Always be aware of the type of conference you are staging, and set appropriate criteria. For example, an incentive event ought to be held somewhere unusual such as at a castle, or in a town or city that delegates have not been to, and which they would consider to be a joy to visit.

Objectives

Do remain conscious of what you want to achieve from this conference. Your venue must help you to fulfil your goals. It may be easier to put over and absorb detailed and complex information in a quiet, academic environment than a lively and distracting one, such as on board a ship.

The Budget

Likewise, be familiar with your overall budget, and how it has been allocated. You must not book a venue which is beyond your financial means – an apparently obvious point perhaps, but one which many organizers seem to ignore, subsequently forcing themselves to cut their expenditure on other, equally important essentials.

The Theme
If you have picked a theme for your conference and want to maintain it through all aspects of the event, you may need to select a venue which will allow you to put up banners and signs and make other amendments to the decor. Some venues will be agreeable to various, superficial changes – others will be less helpful.

Contents
The structure and programme for the conference must have a bearing on your choice of venue as well – perhaps you require one large hall for speeches to address all delegates at the same time, or need several small rooms for related meetings being held alongside the main event.

The location
Think about how far the conference can be held from head office, *and* where speakers and delegates are coming from. Then identify those towns and/or cities that are likely to be acceptable to everyone. Three or four may spring to mind.

The Venue
Work out roughly how many people may attend the event, and the number of seats required. Decide what equipment could be used, and how much space is needed for it. Make a note of any other facilities and services which should be provided by the venue. Figures 3.1 and 3.2 give a list of possible equipment, facilities and services respectively.

Overnight Accommodation
Calculate how many people (and their partners) may stay overnight, the number of rooms needed, and for

Figure 3.1. Useful Equipment

- product display stands
- blackboards
- flip charts
- overhead projectors
- slide projectors
- film projectors
- television sets
- video recorders
- accessories; chalks, pens etc
- spares; bulbs, fuses etc

Figure 3.2. Selected Facilities and Services

- **Business Facilities** — furniture hire
  visual equipment hire
  audio-visual equipment hire
  telephone
  fax
  photocopier
  secretarial support
  other

- **Catering Services** — mid-morning breaks
  lunches
  afternoon breaks
  dinners
  other

- **Leisure Facilities** — bar
  disco
  gymnasium
  hairdresser
  beautician
  swimming pool
  sauna
  solarium
  snooker
  tennis
  squash
  golf
  bowls
  archery
  clay-pigeon shooting
  other

how long. Decide whether the accommodation should be on-site or nearby, and the type and standard of accommodation required. List any facilities and services needed, such as off-street parking and easy access for disabled people.

LOOKING AT LOCATIONS

Having established the criteria against which locations and venues are to be assessed, you can go on to pick the town or city where your conference will be staged. Several trade bodies and publications can provide helpful guidance and information at this stage, as outlined in *Further Reading* and *Useful Addresses*, pages 77 and 79 respectively.

In particular, the British Association of Conference Towns (BACT) offers advice about the 100 or so towns which comprise its membership, and supplies a free publication called the *British Conference Destinations Directory* which describes them in some depth. The *Conference Green Book*, published by Benn Business Information Services Limited and available in many larger libraries, provides data about prospective locations too. When appraising possible sites, you need to look at various, key factors in turn, including the following:

Convenience

You must select a location which is convenient for all – participants should be able to arrive on time feeling relaxed, and reach home at a reasonable hour. Make sure everyone is happy about the location, otherwise some will simply not come, and others will feel disgruntled while they are there.

Transport

The site must not only be convenient in terms of distance, but should have satisfactory road, rail and air links too, as appropriate. Invariably overlooked, there should be sufficient public transport available as well – of prime significance to participants and partners staying over who wish to go out and about.

Attitude
Consider whether the town or city actively tries to encourage conferences to be held there. At the very least, a tourist board should exist which is able to offer advice and assistance as required. As a first-time organizer, you need all the help you can get!

Choice
Be certain that your preferred town or city has a good range of conference venues *and* overnight accommodation to choose from. Naturally, there is no point in picking the perfect location if you cannot find an equally ideal venue in that locality.

Competition
Although probably not yet finalized, you will have a firm idea of when your conference will be staged. Check to see what other events are taking place in the town or city at that time, and decide whether these are a benefit or a drawback for you. They may keep partners occupied during the day *or* they could be a distraction for the participants!

STUDYING VENUES
Once the town or city has been picked, you can move ahead to shortlist venues which are worth visiting. Again, various trade associations and publications can be referred to at this point. BACT and other specialist organizations belonging to the Association of Conference Executives (ACE) and the Meetings Industry Association (MIA) provide a venue location service free, taking your criteria, matching them to potentially ideal venues, and consequently receiving a fee from the chosen venue.

For those who prefer a DIY approach, Benn's *Conference Blue Book* lists 5,000 or more venues throughout the British Isles and details the technical facts and figures which need to be contemplated when composing a shortlist. Here are some of the main areas that you ought to be thinking about:

Locality
Clearly, the venue must be easy to reach *and* find, and satisfactory public transport links should exist to and from the site, especially if participants are staying in overnight accommodation away from the conference itself.

Size
Make sure that the venue is the right size for your conference – big enough for participants and equipment, but not so large that you are paying for unused space. It is surprising how many firms book a huge venue simply to impress and then have to make (false) economies elsewhere because of it.

Facilities and Services
Check that your preferred venue has all of the facilities and services required, perhaps including equipment hire, catering facilities, secretarial support and/or whatever else you need.

Overnight accommodation
You need to be certain that there is suitable overnight accommodation on site or close by, as relevant. Check to see it has the facilities and services which will be expected by participants, such as en-suite facilities and so on.

Timing
Do discover at an early stage whether or not the venue is available on your chosen dates. Find out if there are any

other events being held at the venue at the same time. This is typically overlooked until it is too late to book elsewhere. Make certain that other events being held are compatible with your own. You do not want to find music rehearsals taking place next door when you are trying to speak!

Costs

Add up the likely costs involved with staging your conference at this particular venue, dividing them up between accommodation, equipment, facilities, services and other expenses. Double check what is *and is not* included in the quoted prices. Never exceed your budget, otherwise you will be cutting corners everywhere else.

Assistance

Ideally, the venue will have a track record of staging conferences so that weaknesses and problems have been resolved previously. You do not want them to make mistakes, especially with your money! It would be helpful if there is a conference executive available on site to assist you with your plans.

PAYING A VISIT

It is now sensible to visit perhaps two or three short-listed venues (and separate overnight accommodation if required) to verify the information gathered together already on locality, size and so on, and to make that final choice. Think carefully about the following factors in particular:

The Conference Executive

It is important that the conference executive (or who-ever is assigned to assist you) is experienced and in control, so that you have confidence in him or her. He or she should be able to advise you on your programme, tell you what can and cannot be done at the site and generally be responsive to your needs. Other staff should be equally helpful.

Conference Rooms

In addition to satisfactory dimensions, do check to see that entrances, heights, lengths, widths, obstructions, power points and exits all meet with your approval. Consider lighting, heating and ventilation too, and whether they are acceptable in summer and winter. Think about noise levels, inside and outside the building. Roadworks have unexpectedly interrupted many conferences!

Facilities and Services

Take a (very) good look at what is on offer at the venue, to see that equipment and machinery is in a satisfactory condition and up to date, and if services are up to scratch. Any machines which are difficult to operate should be provided with a technician to help you to work them properly. Find out if you can make changes to the decor as well.

Overnight Accommodation

Likewise, have a close look at the hotel or wherever participants will be staying overnight, to make certain it is of an acceptable standard and that facilities and services are satisfactory. Too often, overnight accommodation is ill-considered, which inevitably results in dissatisfied and unhappy speakers, delegates and partners.

Value For Money

The bottom line when choosing a venue – as in any other business transaction – is whether or not the deal represents value for money, for you and your firm. All things being equal, does this particular venue give you the most for your money? If – or when – you can say 'yes', it is time to proceed.

Before going ahead, ask for the names and telephone numbers of others who have held conferences there. Contact them to hear what they have to say about the venue. If all is well, make a provisional booking outlining your requirements in writing to avoid misunderstandings and confusion. You can firm up and finalize precise details later in accordance with your schedule, once you know the exact numbers attending and so on.

CHECKLIST FOR SUCCESS – THREE

- Have you selected a venue?

- Did you do this by analysing your requirements in terms of the conference objectives, budget, theme, contents, location venue and overnight accommodation?

- Did you look at locations with regard to convenience, transport, attitude, choice of venue and the competition?

- Did you study venues in terms of locality, size, facilities and services, overnight accommodation, timing, costs and the assistance available?

- Did you shortlist venues? What did you think of the conference executive, rooms, facilities and services, overnight accommodation and their value for money?

- Have you made provisional bookings?

STAGE TWO

PROMOTING A CONFERENCE

4. ATTRACTING PARTICIPANTS

Commissioning speakers

Inviting delegates

Publicizing the event

5. BRINGING IN OUTSIDERS

Using specialists

Negotiating with suppliers

Referring to trade bodies

ATTRACTING PARTICIPANTS

Promoting a conference has to be approached carefully, step by step. Attracting participants can be separated out into three important tasks – commissioning speakers, inviting delegates to come to listen to them and publicizing the event to a wider audience. After completing these various activities you can then press ahead to bring in outsiders to help you with your other duties, if or when required.

COMMISSIONING SPEAKERS

Not surprisingly, some considerable thought has to be given to commissioning speakers for your conference. Five main questions spring to mind. Whom do you wish to speak? What do you want them to say? Where will you find them? What will persuade them to attend? How should you invite them? Taking each area in turn:

In-house speakers

Whom do you wish to speak? Inevitably, this depends upon the type of conference, and the message you are putting over. In all probability, you will not be able to choose speakers for certain conferences – the marketing and sales directors intend to speak at a sales conference, the managing director at an incentive event, the firm's PR consultants at a promotional or press conference, and so on. Whether they are good or bad, they are going to talk come what may!

Other speakers

Depending on the conference, its theme, contents, length and budget, you may wish to bring in other speakers from outside your business. Ideally, these should know their subject well, be recognized in their field and be capable of, and experienced at, public speaking and handling discussions. Celebrities are always an attraction, conveying a professional image and adding expertise to an event, but the costs can be prohibitive, certainly running into hundreds if not thousands of pounds for a day's work.

Speeches

What do you want them to say? Realistically, in-house speakers such as your managing director may tell *you* what they are going to talk about and you simply have no choice but to agree with it. Unfortunately, this is often one of the realities of organizing a conference. With outsiders, you have more control, although what they put across should depend upon (and reflect) the theme and message of the event. For example, at a sales conference, the sales director might work through the dry facts and figures, with an independent sales intermediary then motivating everyone with talk of how he or she has been so successful.

Sources

Where will you find them? This and indeed the following questions are easy to answer for in-house speakers. In this instance, they are probably sitting opposite you or are in the office across the corridor! With outsiders, you may need to talk to colleagues, business associates, your own professional association and/or conference trade bodies for contact names, addresses and telephone numbers. See *Useful Addresses*, page 79.

Incentives

Sometimes, you will need to provide an incentive to persuade speakers to come to the conference (although there will also be times when you wish you could persuade the MD or whoever to stay away!). Only you can decide what will motivate, as it depends on the speakers. Some will do it to boost their ego, others just for the money. Other incentives include the chance to meet old friends, make new business acquaintances and visit an unusual location. Identify motivating factors, and stress them when inviting speakers.

Invitations

How should you invite them? There are no hard and fast rules although you should speak on the telephone at an early stage, putting across as much information as possible, and answering questions. If they are agreeable, you should meet to brief them thoroughly, explaining what they are expected to say and do, when, how it fits into the overall programme, and so on. Confirm everything in writing, especially their commitment, fees, expenses and other arrangements. Provide finalized details of the programme later on, checking all is well with another telephone call nearer the time. Meet again at a rehearsal, before the conference begins.

INVITING DELEGATES

When thinking about delegates, you should be aware that most of the questions raised when commissioning speakers are equally applicable here. In particular, whom do you want to invite? Whereabouts are they? What will motivate them to come along? How should they be invited to the event?

Delegates

Whom do you want to invite? Evidently, this is related to the type of conference being staged, *and* what you want to achieve from it. A sales conference may be aimed at in-house sales staff who can boost sales, a press conference at influential members of the media who can publicize your firm. As a rough and ready rule, ask yourself whether the event will help them *and* enable them to assist you in achieving your goals. If so, invite them. If not, try not to – although it is inevitable that you will have to invite some people purely for political reasons.

Locating

It should be relatively easy to locate prospective delegates, especially those who work for your company, or are known to you or your colleagues as customers, business contacts and the like. Your own professional association or trade bodies within the conference industry may also be able to help. See *Useful Addresses*, page 79. Some people may be attracted when you publicize the event within the marketplace – do not underestimate the potential impact of such publicity.

Motivating

What will motivate people to come along? Some delegates such as staff will feel obliged to attend whether they want to or not (although it is obviously best to have an enthusiastic audience, so try to make them interested too). Others may have to be persuaded to come, and can be motivated in numerous ways. Your company's reputation, exciting speakers, an interesting theme, a convenient time, a pleasant location and a rich and varied programme can help – certainly far more than the free bottles of wine and prize draws which some organizers consider to be of key importance.

Contacting

An attractive invitation is helpful as well. Whether you approach would-be delegates face-to-face, on the telephone or by letter, you need to make the conference sound appealing. Tell them why it is being held, what it involves, why they should attend *and* how they will benefit from it – they need to know that their visit will be worthwhile, and not a waste of time. Mention those features which you feel will attract them most of all – the theme, the chance to meet and talk to your celebrity speaker and so forth.

PUBLICIZING THE EVENT

Having commissioned speakers from inside and/or outside your company and invited key delegates to the conference, you can set about promoting the event to the outside world. This is all good publicity for your firm, showing everyone that you are a go-ahead concern, addressing important issues, etc. Also, other speakers and delegates may come forward as a result of these activities, which could be helpful. There are several reliable ways of publicizing your conference, including the following:

Press releases

Press releases of the 'who-what-when-where-why' variety can be sent to consumer and trade newspapers and magazines which are familiar with your company, products and services, and may be happy to run a feature on your conference. If forwarded to the Association of Conference Executives (ACE), it might incorporate details in its monthly 'What's on' calendar, which can be beneficial too. (See *Useful Addresses*, page 79.)

Directories

It may be a good idea to pay a small fee to have an entry placed in an appropriate trade directory, most notably *Conferences and Exhibitions Diary* in the conference industry. (See *Further Reading*, page 77.) Inclusion in this particular directory should make sure that everyone involved in or associated with conferences will be aware of your forthcoming event. You may know of other directories in your profession which are worth contacting as well.

Advertising

You might also want to spend money on general advertising in the press and other media, if your budget permits this and you believe it is worthwhile in your circumstances. If you do, your professional or trade journal might be an obvious choice. So too might be *Conference and Exhibition Fact Finder*, the trade magazine for the conference marketplace. This is read by the majority of people working in and around the conference industry. (See *Further Reading*, page 77.)

CHECKLIST FOR SUCCESS – FOUR

- Have you commissioned speakers for your conference?

- Did you think about in-house and outside speakers and the speeches they should make before finding and asking them to participate?

- Have you invited delegates to the event?

- Did you contemplate who the right delegates are, before locating and persuading them to attend?

- Have you publicized the conference, perhaps in press releases, directories and other advertising media?

5

BRINGING IN OUTSIDERS

The potential value of bringing in outsiders to help you should not be underestimated – on occasions, they can make the difference between a successful and an unsuccessful conference. It is worthwhile stepping back to consider using specialists, negotiating with suppliers and referring to trade bodies for assistance, especially if you are a first time organizer having to do this work in addition to your usual activities.

USING SPECIALISTS

Professional conference organizers (PCOs) do exist in the United Kingdom, although they are relatively few in number. Reputable ones tend to belong to the Association of Conference Executives (ACE) which can provide you with a relevant list, on request. (See *Useful Addresses*, page 79.) Think about the pluses and minuses of using such a specialist before deciding whether to employ one in some capacity, or to continue to go it alone.

Pluses

Quite simply, a professional will (or certainly should) know exactly what he or she is doing, having done everything many times before. He or she can advise on or handle such matters as budgeting, scheduling, booking a suitable venue, choosing and approaching speakers and delegates, hiring and/or buying equipment and so on, through to evaluating the conference. By taking over some of the more time-consuming and/or difficult tasks, the conference organizer will save you time, effort *and* money – as you will almost certainly make a few costly mistakes first time around.

Minuses

Obviously, the main minus of employing a specialist is the cost (although this needs to be weighed carefully against the time and efficiency savings, *and* any discounts that he or she may be able to negotiate better than you). Often ignored, another minus is that regardless of how good they are, these professionals can never know as much about your firm as you do, nor are they as committed as you are to getting it right. Hands-on knowledge and commitment are hard to transfer to outsiders, whatever they might say.

The Choice

Your decision to work with a professional or not depends on many factors, not least your experience in this field, plus time and financial constraints. If you are inexperienced in certain areas and/or have limited time available to you *and* can incorporate the fees in your budget, then you will probably wish to commission a specialist for some assistance. Alternatively, you may feel that you have what it takes to carry on alone, in your careful, step-by-step manner. Why not? There is no reason why you cannot be just as successful on your own.

NEGOTIATING WITH SUPPLIERS

If you decide to continue with your DIY approach, you will need to think about negotiating with various organizations and individuals – most notably, those supplying you with a venue, visual and audio-visual equipment, other facilities and services, and so forth. Even if you are handing over some tasks to a professional conference organizer, you should still consider the do's and don'ts of negotiating so that you can strike the best possible deal with the particular specialist! Let's look at the steps in sequence:

Supplies

Clearly, you have to calculate what your firm is providing for the conference, and what is being supplied by outsiders. Much will depend on the type of conference being staged, where it will be held, what the message is, how it will be put across, and so on. As an example, perhaps your business is providing the venue, speakers and delegates for a sales conference, but wishes to hire some additional audio–visual equipment and arrange catering services too.

Suppliers

Next, you have to work out who your suppliers might be, and the qualities they should possess. Not surprisingly, these qualities will differ from one to another – an equipment supplier needs to provide usable, up-to-date machines, a caterer fresh and tasty food, and so forth. Nonetheless, you should identify what you want from each of them. By and large, you will possibly be looking for suppliers who have a sound knowledge and experience of their field, products and services and the conference industry, a genuine interest in your needs and competitive prices. Perhaps they ought to be reputable, trustworthy and helpful too. It is up to you.

Go Betweens

You may already have a list of potential suppliers who meet your criteria which has developed from your normal day-to-day dealings, or from recommendations from colleagues and other business contacts. Alternatively – and to ensure that suppliers have a proper understanding of the particular characteristics of conferences – refer to trade bodies and publications for a contacts list. See *Further Reading* and *Useful Addresses*, pages 77 and 79.

The Negotiations

Again, negotiations will vary according to circumstances, although a few universal guidelines are worthy of consideration. Approach at least three shortlisted suppliers for each facility or service required. Meet, tell them exactly what you want, look at their work and see how well they fulfil your criteria. Hear what they have to say, and note their prices. Obtain the names and addresses of previous clients, and take up references. Detail everything in writing for your chosen suppliers – the precise brief, workload and schedule, payment arrangements and so on. Other would-be suppliers should be thanked and rejected politely.

REFERRING TO TRADE BODIES

In all probability, you will already have referred to trade bodies such as the British Association of Conference Towns (BACT) when choosing a venue and the Association of Conference Executives (ACE) when selecting a professional conference organizer. Without doubt, you will continue to contact them time and again as you run, and subsequently evaluate, the conference. You might also want to think about becoming a member of some of them. Do be aware of the benefits and drawbacks of seeking such advice though.

Benefits

The main benefit is that trade bodies are usually a first class source of reference, able to put you in touch with the organizations and individuals you want to talk to. Should you deal with their members, you know that they have agreed to abide by codes of conduct, which implies (but does not absolutely guarantee) high standards and ethical behaviour. If you are dissatisfied and have a complaint, the relevant body should help you to settle the matter, dismissing the member in extreme cases.

Drawbacks

The major drawback here is that trade organizations represent their members and exist primarily to promote their interests and to increase trade for them. Thus, their advice and assistance is not as independent and unbiased as some people seem to think or want it to be.

Decent and honourable though they are, trade bodies will recommend their members, although other, non-members may be equally good. Even in trade publications, entries have been paid for by specialists and suppliers, so they are not independent either. Do not forget this.

Joining Up
Working on the 'if you can't beat 'em, join 'em' principle, it may be a good idea to think about becoming a member of such bodies as the Meetings Industry Association (MIA). In return for a membership fee and adherence to its trading standards, you will be eligible to receive its advice and various other benefits such as discounts on its training courses and other members' services. (See *Useful Addresses*, page 79.)

CHECKLIST FOR SUCCESS – FIVE

- Have you considered using conference specialists?

- Did you assess the pluses and minuses before making a choice?

- Have you contemplated negotiating with suppliers?

- Did you think about the supplies and suppliers needed, the go-betweens and the do's and don'ts of negotiations?

- Have you referred to trade bodies?

- Did you appraise the benefits and drawbacks before reaching that decision?

6

WORKING WITH SPEAKERS

Pulling together all of your various organizational and promotional activities in order to run a successful conference is not a simple task – and there will be times when you wish you did not have to be the one to do it! Working well with your speakers is crucially important, so you need to know something about speaking in public, staging rehearsals and implementing changes to your programme, usually at the last minute.

SPEAKING IN PUBLIC

Although you have been given the job of staging this event, it is unlikely that you are also expected to speak at it, other than perhaps introducing speakers to the audience, and possibly making a brief closing speech as well. However, it is sensible to have an idea of how to speak in public so that you can complete these duties properly. Whatever you have to do, you must plan, prepare and rehearse:

Planning

When planning any speech, you need to answer various questions. Why are you speaking? Probably, you are acting as a link, to move the programme on quietly and unobtrusively – you are not there to upstage the speakers! What do you want to achieve? Be aware of your goals: to introduce a speaker who is unknown to the audience, to thank him or her for an interesting speech, and so on. Who is in your audience? You should be conscious of whom you are addressing, perhaps an in-house crowd who can be warmed up with a joke, or outsiders who expect a formal and respectful introduction. What do they want? Invariably, they want you to shut up so the session can commence. So be brief!

Preparing

Mindful of your answers to these questions, you can set about drafting speeches in skeleton form. To introduce a speaker, you might make a note of his or her name, background and expertise, what will be talked about and so on. To thank someone, you could jot down notes about thanking them warmly, highlighting one or two valuable statements made which are worth stressing, and encouraging another round of applause before going on to the next speaker or break, as appropriate. Prepare no more than a framework of key words and phrases for each speech which can then be transferred onto small cards for reference on the day. Fully written speeches are unwise – they are difficult to adhere to word for word, and harm the flow and spontaneity of your comments.

Rehearsing

Always rehearse what you have to say – initially, on your own in front of a mirror, or preferably on video for a subsequent, more reflective assessment. Try to relax and be yourself so that you sound natural and sincere. It is wise to maintain eye contact on a regular, roving basis with your audience, to build rapport. Do keep control of your body movements – waving hands, tapping feet and striding back and forth are all very distracting. It is sensible to practise with any equipment you may be using, to make sure you can handle it without mishaps. Present your speeches in front of two or three people whom you respect – they should help you to polish up your performance.

STAGING REHEARSALS

Ideally, you briefed the speakers, venue, suppliers and so forth early on, subsequently finalizing details and checking all was in order in good time for the conference. Some time before the event – a day, a week or whenever suits you – it is a good idea to hold a full rehearsal to spot weaknesses and problems which may need to be dealt with before it all begins. Work through your planned programme in its correct sequence, paying special attention to the following areas:

Speakers

Sit and listen to speakers making speeches, presentations, leading discussions and handling questions and answer sessions, with you acting as the audience. Do they put across the right message, whether an informative or inspirational one? Alternatively, do they ramble, or stray off course, perhaps on to their pet subject? Are they good at what they do, adhering loosely to the basic do's and don'ts of successful speaking? Even the best speakers – and hopefully you have chosen these – can benefit from a helpful suggestion here and there. They may have a tendency to repeat the same phrase over and again, or have a mannerism which irritates after a while.

Contents

Think carefully about the order and mix of the contents of your programme. Now that you can see it unfolding, do you feel it is structured in a logical manner? Have you achieved a good balance between business and pleasure? Are the timings of the different sessions about right, or do speakers stop short of or over-run their allocated times? It is rare that a programme sketched out on paper transfers perfectly into practice, without some changes needing to be made either to its running order and/or timings. You would have to be a genius to get it spot on, particularly first time around.

Venue

Certainly, you should have made a close and thorough inspection of the venue some time ago, but you will probably need to pay further attention to it again now that the practicalities are under way. Have entrances, heights, lengths, widths and so on proved to be satisfactory? Can banners, signs and other display materials be fixed up easily? Will delegates really be comfortable, and be able to see and hear everything that is going on? Bear in mind in rehearsals that an audience of one can see and hear much more than a full-to-capacity audience will do on the day – so make allowances for this.

Facilities and Services

Take the opportunity to discover how good the facilities and services are. Has the venue supplied the facilities it said it would? Are you absolutely happy with them? What about outside suppliers? Are their services satisfactory? Almost inevitably, some facilities and services will not be up to scratch, ranging from a faulty piece of equipment to tea being provided instead of tea *and* coffee as requested. Even more worrying are facilities and services which are unavailable now but which are promised for the conference itself. Typically, the secretary who is supplying administrative support is off sick but will be 'back in time'. Attend to these problems immediately, and keep working until you are happy with them. Don't adopt an 'it'll be alright on the night' approach – it rarely is.

Miscellaneous Concerns

Keep a watchful eye on all of those apparently trivial and mundane matters which are so often overlooked, but which can help to make a success of the event. As examples, do speakers have a carafe of water at hand in case they need a drink? Will delegates have pads and pencils available should they wish to make notes? Is saccharin on offer when tea and coffee are provided? Attempt to spot irritating little problems such as these during rehearsals, so that they can be remedied by the time the event begins in earnest.

IMPLEMENTING CHANGES

You will be very fortunate if you do not have to make some last-minute changes to your conference programme. More likely, your rehearsals will highlight various shortcomings and accidents waiting to happen. The following are some of the more common problems which tend to occur, and possible ways of resolving them:

Over-running

There will always be at least one speaker who runs over the allocated time – unfortunately, it will probably be the managing director, who is a law unto himself, or herself! In theory, this is easy to remedy – the speaker may need to be asked to stick to the script rather than meander off, or perhaps that script could be tightened up without weakening its message or key points. There may be some unnecessary repetition, or one of the anecdotes may be cut out. In practice, telling some speakers what to do is difficult, and you might have to resort to some form of signal to indicate how long the MD or whoever has left to speak.

Under-running

Conversely, a speaker may finish before the agreed time, leaving everything in limbo for the remaining period. Perhaps he or she has gabbled through the script, and needs to relax, take it easy and slow down. Possibly, one or two points have been missed out or have not been covered in enough detail, or an anecdote needs to be added to personalize a rather dry, robotic talk. Alternatively, it might be beneficial to set aside the outstanding time for questions and answers, an examination of a product or a general discussion, which may help to increase understanding and re-inforce the message.

Unbalanced

It is hard to mix business and pleasure together well, and some first-time organizers try to cram as many business activities into a conference as they can – quite an ordeal for delegates! If you begin to feel restless, bored and irritated during rehearsals, then you can be absolutely certain that delegates will feel the same (if not far worse) on the day itself. Get a better balance by jiggling the order so that (endless) speeches are separated by demonstrations, questions and answers and the like – participation and interaction help to sustain and build interest. Break up long sessions into two or three units, giving delegates time for a drink, cigarette or visit to the loo!

Supplies

Without doubt, you will be unhappy with certain aspects of the venue's facilities and the equipment and other services provided by suppliers – perhaps the chairs are uncomfortable, a flip chart is torn and dirty, felt-tipped pens dry up during use, and so on. Not surprisingly, all of these minor shortcomings can combine to create a poor impression on the delegates. Whatever the problems, deal with them personally and do not rely on anyone else, as they may not share your commitment to the event. Get the chairs changed by the venue or make alternative arrangements (which should be reflected in the venue's bill). Oversee all changes yourself – this is a time-consuming nuisance, but should at least ensure the conference runs smoothly.

CHECKLIST FOR SUCCESS – SIX

- Have you spoken well in public?

- Did you plan, prepare and rehearse fully?

- Have you staged rehearsals?

- Did you address speakers, contents, the venue, facilities, services and any other miscellaneous concerns?

- Have you implemented any changes, perhaps to speeches, the mix between business and pleasure, or supplies?

7

HANDLING EQUIPMENT

Inevitably, you and your speakers will wish to use equipment of some kind within the conference programme, when making speeches, conducting presentations, leading discussions, or whatever. Thus, you should contemplate including visual and audio–visual aids in the event, and be aware of how to make the most of the equipment chosen. It can enhance or ruin a presentation, and therefore needs to be treated with respect and care so that it has a positive impact.

INCLUDING VISUAL AIDS

There are a whole host of visual aids to choose from, which are used regularly in different types of conference – both successfully *and* unsuccessfully. Here are some of the most popular ones available:

Product Displays

It is obviously a good idea to display the goods that you are talking about at a promotional, press, trade or training event, to support and substantiate your message. Alternatively, if they are too large and bulky for the venue or are costly to transport and set up, consider using models or samples instead. The ability to see, touch, taste and examine products has a powerful and memorable impact on delegates.

Flip Charts

These successors to old–fashioned blackboards tend to be inexpensive, informal and well suited to transferring detailed information to smaller groups of delegates who can sit close enough to see what is written on them. However, their informality and rather intimate nature means that they are less suitable for more formal and larger events where they often appear amateurish.

Thus, they may be appropriate at smaller, in-house sales, incentive or training conferences, but are not so relevant at promotional, press and trade events for the outside world.

Overhead Projectors

OHPs – as they are more commonly referred to – are similar in many respects to flip charts. They are cheap to use, fairly unpretentious, and ideal for passing on data to smaller numbers of in-house delegates, but they are unsuitable for larger numbers of outsiders who may expect a rather more upmarket, hi-tech presentation. A minor drawback – unless it applies to you – is that some speakers seem to find it difficult to talk and operate an OHP at the same time, stumbling over leads, putting acetates on upside down and so forth.

Slides

With their vivid and colourful pictures, these usually convey a professional and polished image of the firm and its goods and services to internal and external audiences. As their size can be varied on a screen, you can show them to many delegates, certainly far more than with flip charts and OHPs. Nonetheless, they are relatively costly to produce, have to be seen in a darkened room, which reduces speaker-delegate contact, and are less suited to putting over in-depth details. Also, they can be fiddly to operate, with the added danger of slides being in the wrong order, back to front, upside down, and the like.

Handouts

Too often disregarded by speakers at conferences, handouts summarizing the key points of a speech or presentation have many advantages. They are cheap and easy to print, enable quite detailed and complex information to be put across, and perhaps most important of all, allow delegates to listen rather than make notes during the programme. The main disadvantage is that they have a 'college lecture' image which some delegates may find offputting – so money may have to be spent upgrading 'student notes' into 'executive resources'!

INCORPORATING AUDIO-VISUAL AIDS

Similarly, there are numerous audio-visual aids incorporated into conferences nowadays, some of which are extremely sophisticated and impressive. The following are probably the most common ones on the market:

Slides with Sound

It is not unknown at conferences for slides to be shown alongside a running sound commentary, either prepared in-house or by an outside supplier. In addition to the other advantages of using slides, it means the 'perfect' speech can be heard, without coughs, hesitations and errors. This is fine in theory but the almost inevitable drawback is that it is difficult to synchronize the audio and visual elements – sometimes with embarrassing results, which reflect badly on your professionalism.

Films

The use of a film and soundtrack is popular. In its favour, it offers colour, movement, the ability to demonstrate, quality speech and music – all in all, a highly polished, memorable aid, shown to in-house delegates or outsiders at any event. Against it is the cost of having a relevant film produced on your behalf, which is often prohibitively expensive. Also, films tend to stand alone, dominating the programme and not allowing two-way communication to occur, which is rarely beneficial to the overall impression of the conference.

Videos

In many respects, videos offer similar pluses and minuses to films, especially those which are made specifically for your company to use at this and other events. Perhaps the key difference is that many ready-made videos are purchased by conference organizers to show during training sessions, most notably those featuring John Cleese, Mel Smith and Griff Rhys Jones. Excellent though these are (and relatively inexpensive too), it is important to remember that they may not have the same theme, message and emphasis as your conference, which may confuse delegates. Also, the audience tend to recall John Cleese, or whoever, rather than the points being made.

MAKING THE MOST OF EQUIPMENT

In order to make the right choice and use of visual and audio–visual aids, you should be conscious of their benefits and drawbacks, before contemplating other factors which are likely to influence your decisions.

Benefits

Such aids can help to put across a message better. For example, it is easier to show charts of statistics on an OHP than read out every figure. It saves time too. They can also add variety to a lengthy speech, which may maintain interest and enthusiasm, and increase the possibility that delegates will absorb and retain a message for longer. As an example, seeing and touching a product or looking at a colour slide or film of it will stay in the memory far longer than a spoken description will ever do.

Drawbacks

Of course, arranging visual and audio–visual aids requires time, effort and money. Too often, they then take over – most delegates will be painfully familiar with speakers who do no more than stand back and read out what is on the OHP sheet or who shout out pointless explanatory comments about what is being seen on film. Sometimes, aids are just not relevant, being introduced as speakers feel they should have something to fill out a speech, or because rivals use them. As significant, not all speakers can handle equipment comfortably, and occasionally it breaks down, inevitably at the worst possible moment.

Choosing

Clearly, the aids you choose will depend on your situation. The most prominent influence must be your audience. Are you addressing a small number of in-house delegates in a relaxed and informal atmosphere or large numbers of outsiders, stiff-backed and formal. So what should you pick? Consider the message, speakers and the length of each session. Is this a pep talk, or the exchange of nitty gritty data? What aids should you select? Think about your budget. Can you afford to spend money in this area? Is it really necessary?

Using

Whatever you choose to use, do remember that these are *aids*, not substitutes for speakers. Do not have too many, or allow them to dominate the proceedings. Make sure they look suitably professional and are easy to handle – otherwise speakers will appear unprofessional. If appropriate, have a technician on hand to operate equipment, especially if it is complex or distracting for speakers to use. It is worth stressing that all aids must be checked and double-checked beforehand to make certain they are working properly. Always have spares available – pens for flip charts, bulbs for OHPs and so on.

CHECKLIST FOR SUCCESS – SEVEN

- Have you included visual aids in the programme – product displays, flip charts, overhead projectors, slides, handouts?

- Have you incorporated audio-visual aids too – slides with sound, films, video?

- Have you made the most of the equipment available?

- Did you recognise the benefits and drawbacks of various aids before choosing and using them?

8

LOOKING AFTER PARTICIPANTS

For your conference to be truly successful, you do need to look after all of the participants – and these include speakers, delegates *and* their partners. Too often, partners are overlooked, which may cause anger and offence. It is wise to know as much as possible about taking care of delegates, managing miscellaneous matters and entertaining everyone before, during and after the event.

TAKING CARE OF DELEGATES

Having invited delegates to the conference, received replies and probably liaised with them further at some stage to confirm various details and arrangements, it is tempting to sit back and wait for them to arrive, keen and enthusiastic to join your programme. This is an understandable feeling, as you have many other tasks and duties to perform. Nevertheless, it is more sensible to pay special attention to delegates' requirements. If you wish them to react in the ways you want – to place sales orders and so on – you have to take care of them, and their needs.

Pre-conference Documents

Your invitation will have set down numerous details, subsequently confirmed by you on request, either in writing or (more likely) on the telephone. Additional documents can then be sent out at regular intervals between the invitation and the event, in order to inform, advise and most important of all, to maintain interest and the desire to attend. Typically, these will include such items as a finalized programme (again stressing the benefits of attendance), tickets and paperwork (relating to admission to the conference and overnight accommodation) and a map (highlighting the precise locations of the venue, overnight accommodation, car parks and local places of interest).

Travel and Accommodation

Your pre-conference materials will have incorporated travel and accommodation arrangements, whether delegates are expected to make their own way to the venue or be taken by coaches running from head office, and so forth. In addition to the obvious details – coach departure times, hotel booking-in procedures, meal times and the like – it is important that delegates are made aware of what is (and is not) included in the arrangements, and being paid for by your company. For example, sales representatives attending a conference may think that drinks purchased at the hotel bar can be charged to the conference account. If this is not so, tell them in advance!

Conference Packs

Many organizers arrange to have conference packs handed out to delegates on arrival. These might contain further details about the programme, speakers and social activities as well as sales facts and figures, product information, trade news and whatever else is relevant to this particular type of event. Clearly, this is a good idea as it provides delegates with all the data needed to participate fully in the conference. Whatever you do, give them time to read material before the programme begins. Don't send packs out to delegates beforehand though – the postage and packing often exceeds the printing costs and some of them will be mislaid or left behind by delegates.

Badges

These are important for security purposes – they help to ensure that only invited delegates are able to attend, as visitors not wearing them can be stopped, checked and turned away, if appropriate. Choose badges that can be clipped to lapels or pockets as they usually cause less damage to clothing than ones with pins or sticky backs. Make certain that delegates' names and those of the companies they represent are printed boldly on them, so they can be read easily. Do double-check that names are spelt correctly as misspellings can upset people. Hand out badges on arrival with the conference packs – never send them off in advance as most are lost or left behind.

Conference Rooms

So far as delegates are concerned, they want to see and hear everything, and feel comfortable while they are in the conference – obvious perhaps, although these basic requirements seem to be overlooked or ignored at some events. You do not need to do much to keep them happy – have enough chairs, make sure they are pleasant to sit in and have plenty of legroom and easy access to gangways. Give delegates a clear view of what is going on, and make speakers speak up! Restrict smoking to (brief but regular) breaks, and have some fresh air circulating, if possible.

Hotel Rooms

By and large, delegates want much the same from their hotel rooms, if they are staying overnight. They wish to be able to relax in pleasant and amenable surroundings – clean and comfortable beds, en-suite facilities, space, tea and coffee making equipment, a television and radio, a desk to work at, a telephone, room service, perhaps a nice view, and so on. It is worth stressing again that delegates must know what they can *and* cannot put on to the conference bill – otherwise those 'phones will be in constant use!

MANAGING MISCELLANEOUS MATTERS

Not surprisingly, there are numerous miscellaneous tasks and duties which need to be attended to at the conference, to ensure that speakers, delegates and the programme are well co-ordinated, and the event runs without a hitch. These are some of the main areas of concern:

Registration

It is sensible to have a registration desk or area by the entrance to the venue or conference room, as appropriate. This should be staffed by one or (more likely) two of your assistants. It serves as a focal point where delegates' names can be ticked off a list on arrival, literature and badges can be handed out, messages and mislaid items collected and passed on. Any problems, and speakers, delegates and suppliers will head there – so make certain that those assistants know exactly what they are doing!

Display Material

Hopefully, you found out at an early stage whether or not you could put up banners, signs, sashes and the like and checked that everything was in order during your rehearsals. Nonetheless, keep any eye on any display areas and contents on an ongoing basis, to ensure they continue to look fresh and clean, and are a credit to your company. Do have spare materials available, just in case the originals are damaged. Car parking spaces should be signed as well so that everyone knows where *and* where not to park – an apparently trivial point, until arguments start between participants and other guests at the venue.

Security

It is possible that security may be an issue at this event. Typically, competitors might attempt to infiltrate a sales conference to find out about your current performance and forthcoming plans. Strict registration procedures, an insistence that badges are worn on lapels and polite but firm checks on unidentified people coming into the conference room are essential. As important when expensive items are on the premises are constant vigilance and a willingness to stop and ask people who they are and what they are doing when these items are being moved about.

Safety

The venue should have its own well-rehearsed procedures for accidents and emergencies – and you need to know what they are *and* what you should do in the event of a fire, bomb alert and so on. Make sure that key personnel and speakers are aware of the arrangements too. If or when a crisis occurs, delegates will look to you, or whoever is talking to them at the time, for clear and specific instructions.

Insurance

When you drafted your schedule, you will have made a note of insurance and subsequently negotiated cover with your firm's insurers in case of the event having to be cancelled, or other emergencies. Mindful of security and safety at the conference, it is worth thinking about again. It is particularly important that you are covered for damage to or loss of equipment and against accidents and injuries to speakers, delegates *and* partners. Of course, the venue and hotel providing overnight accommodation will be insured, but check to see exactly what their cover is – you may need to add to that cover to protect yourself.

Assistance

As the person responsible for setting up the conference, you will probably have carried out almost all of the work to date on your own, albeit with the occasional chat to colleagues, meetings with superiors and advice from trade associations and suppliers. However, it will be apparent by now – if not some time ago – that you need assistance to keep everything ticking over. Make certain you have well-informed, conscientious assistants on hand to help you welcome people, deal with queries, fetch, carry and attend to 101 other duties. Give yourself a break – you deserve one!

ENTERTAINING EVERYONE

Not surprisingly, time and financial constraints force many organizers to squeeze as much business into a conference as possible, leaving little room for a social programme of any kind. Although this is natural, it is wiser to make an effort to keep everyone entertained, otherwise they will probably become tired and dispirited and far less likely to do as you want them to do – to take in updated information, place sales orders, promote a new product, or whatever. Much can be done to entertain delegates, speakers and their partners, including the following:

Breaks

It can be a good idea to start the programme with a break! Daft though this may sound, it does give everyone the chance to arrive, chat, mingle and get to know each other in a social atmosphere. Also, it means that the conference can begin on time, without subsequent interruptions from latecomers. Regular breaks throughout the programme are important so that everyone can take a breather and socialize with their colleagues – encourage them to do this by providing them with a choice of light refreshments, a sufficient number of comfortable chairs to sit in (if they have to stand up during sessions) and room to stand (if they have to remain seated at other times).

Lunches

Whether you begin an event with a lunch or have one in the middle of a programme, there are a few guidelines which are worth consideration. Keep it light and alcohol-free if you want speakers and delegates to stay bright and alert for the remainder of the day. Do take account of participants' special needs and diets – some may be vegetarians, others diabetics, and so on. A buffet lunch should comprise easy-to-handle, bite-sized foods which can be collected easily, without having to queue. If lunch is served to seated participants, make certain that service is prompt, quiet and efficient. (It is at times like this that your preparation – visiting venues, taking up references and the like – is really useful.)

Dinners

A formal dinner should be held only at the end of an event, when there is more time to relax and enjoy it. Do bring everybody together – speakers, delegates *and* partners – for this occasion, which may perhaps be highlighted by presentations to top salespeople and even followed by a cabaret or dancing to a band. As with lunches, the menu must take account of participants' tastes and wishes, and the service must be swift and discreet. Many presentations have been marred by the clatterings of waiters and waitresses.

Organized Activities

In addition to catering arrangements, you may wish to set up various other activities for speakers' and delegates' partners during the days, and for everyone in the evenings. Perhaps partners can be taken by coach to a local tourist attraction or other special events in the area, such as a garden show. Participants and partners can join in with (not too demanding or competitive) quizzes, games and competitions after each day's programme has concluded. These can help to foster a good team spirit and harmony between everybody. Whatever you arrange, make sure they are optional and un-embarrassing – some people will not wish to participate, others will but will not want to look foolish.

Other Activities

Of course, there will be occasions when speakers, delegates and partners do not wish to be entertained – perhaps they dislike a particular activity, would prefer to chat to friends they have not seen for some time or simply wish to relax on their own or with their partners. Hopefully, you chose a venue and/or overnight accommodation which provide facilities that enable them to entertain themselves – at a bar, solarium, snooker room, on a squash court, in a swimming pool, and so on.

The Right Blend

It is not easy to achieve the correct blend of entertainments – as always, it is up to you to decide what is right in your circumstances. There are many influential factors, not least the type of conference you are staging, its programme and length and the numbers and types of participants in attendance. A three-day incentive event for leading salespeople and their partners may incorporate almost all of these entertainments, an afternoon press conference for local media representatives little more than tea and biscuits. Your needs may fall midway between these two extremes.

CHECKLIST FOR SUCCESS – EIGHT

- Have you taken care of delegates?

- Did you provide them with pre-conference documents, arrange travel and accommodation, give them conference packs and badges, and make sure that their conference and hotel rooms were satisfactory?

- Have you managed miscellaneous matters well?

- Did you attend to such areas as registration, display material, security, safety, insurance and assistance for yourself?

- Have you entertained everyone, including partners?

- Did you arrange breaks, lunches, dinners, organized and other activities, as appropriate? Was the blend right?

EVALUATING A CONFERENCE

9. REVIEWING THE EVENT

Considering organizational activities

Thinking about promotional techniques

Assessing your tactics

10. FOLLOWING THROUGH

Writing a report

Improving yourself

Planning ahead

REVIEWING THE EVENT

Evaluating a conference is important – too often it is judged to be a success or a failure without any careful thought or detailed analysis at all. Reviewing the event should comprise three key stages – considering your organizational activities, thinking about your promotional techniques, and assessing your tactics at the conference. Only by reviewing your conference in this way will you really be able to decide whether it was successful, or not.

CONSIDERING ORGANIZATIONAL ACTIVITIES

To begin with, you should sit down and look back over all of the organizational tasks and duties which you carried out when you were first given the responsibility of staging the event, six, nine, twelve months ago, or whenever. You made some preliminary plans before going on to draft out a programme and select a venue which would be suitable for the event:

Your Plans

Did you identify your conference? Most likely, it was a mix of several types rolled into one. Did you recognize your goals? Look at each of them in turn to see if you have achieved them. In particular, have delegates done what you wanted them to do – promoted goods, placed orders for them, or whatever? Did you establish a budget? In retrospect, decide whether it was sufficient for your needs. Did you adhere to it? Just as significant, contemplate whether you maintained a satisfactory cash flow as well.

Your Programme

Did you pick a theme? If so, was it a specific and easy to understand one which was attractive to participants?

Consider whether the advantages of that theme out-weighed any disadvantages. What about the contents of your programme? Were they relevant, interesting, balanced and brief? Think about the feedback from participants, to work out if it went down well with them. How about your schedule? Did it unfold as expected, allowing you enough time to do everything properly, and at the right times?

The Venue

Did you analyse your requirements? Study each of them in sequence. Was the right locality chosen? See if it fulfilled your criteria concerning location. Did you pick the right venue and overnight accommodation? Again, see if they met your requirements. Did you pay a visit to shortlisted venues, *and* take up references? With the benefit of hindsight, decide whether or not your first impressions were accurate.

THINKING ABOUT PROMOTIONAL TECHNIQUES

Think back over the ways in which you promoted the conference to speakers, delegates and others in the conference industry and the outside world. All of your varied promotional actions can probably be grouped together into two overall activities – attracting participants and bringing in outsiders.

Participants

Were you happy with your speakers? Hopefully, you were able to find and invite the correct mix of in-house and other speakers who put across the right messages for you. What about the delegates? Did you locate, contact and motivate the right delegates to attend the event? If they have not promoted/bought your products, or whatever, then they were probably the wrong delegates! Did you publicize the event well? Mull over your use of press releases, directories and advertising. Did other, *suitable* speakers and delegates come forward as a result of this publicity?

Outsiders

Did you use a professional conference organizer to assist you? If so, was he or she really helpful? If you did not employ one, how did you cope on your own? What about suppliers? Consider whether you made the right choices, negotiated well with them and were satisfied with the facilities and services provided. Did you refer to (or even join) trade bodies? If you did, was their advice and guidance useful? Did they help you to avoid making mistakes? If you did not refer to (or join) them, do you wish that you had done? Could some mistakes have been avoided?

ASSESSING YOUR TACTICS

Contemplate your tactics at the conference itself, to see how well it was run after all of those months of preparation and promotion. You will have worked with speakers, handled equipment and looked after participants – hopefully, with some success!

Speakers

Did you speak well in public? Think about how your opening and closing speeches were received. Find out if your colleagues agree with your assessment. How did the rehearsals go? Were they beneficial? They should have enabled you to spot problems and other, minor concerns *before* rather than during the programme itself. Did you make any changes at the last moment? If so, what did you do? Consider whether they had the desired effects, or not.

Equipment

Were visual aids included in the programme? Appraise the use of product displays, flip charts, overhead projectors, slides and handouts. Decide if they were helpful. Did you incorporate audio–visual aids too? Assess the use of slides with sound, films and videos. Conclude whether they were useful. Was the right mix of visual and audio-visual equipment chosen in the circumstances? It is important to contemplate if these items *aided* speakers, or simply blurred and confused their messages.

Participants

Did you really take care of your delegates well? You should have supplied them with pre-conference documents, conference packs and badges, attended to travel and accommodation arrangements and provided first class conference and hotel rooms. What do they think? Did you manage miscellaneous matters properly? Mull over what you did with regard to registrations, display materials, security, safety and the like. Did you get it right? Was everyone kept entertained, especially partners? Think over the breaks, lunches, dinner, organized and other activities. Did they prove to be popular?

Having looked at all of these areas, gathered together your own thoughts, talked to speakers, delegates and partners and conferred with colleagues, you should be in a better position to make an overall, balanced judgement of the event. Some mistakes are inevitable, especially first time, but if you kept to your budget, ran a relatively smooth conference which was generally praised *and* achieved your objectives then you are entitled to consider it to have been a success. Perhaps not quite the 'perfect' conference though – that comes next time, now you have learned from this experience!

CHECKLIST FOR SUCCESS – NINE

- Have you reviewed the event thoroughly?

- Did you consider your organizational activities in terms of your plans, programme and venue?

- Did you then think about your promotional techniques with regard to participants and outsiders?

- Did you assess your tactics at the conference in relation to speakers, equipment and participants?

- Was the event a success?

FOLLOWING THROUGH

Having reviewed the conference in some depth and reached a favourable conclusion, it is tempting to stop work immediately and return to your usual tasks and duties. Nevertheless, it is wise to do a little more to lay the foundations for a perfect conference next time around. To do this, you need to write a report, improve yourself and plan ahead.

WRITING A REPORT

All of the knowledge and experience you have gained from setting up this event is in danger of being lost if it is not transferred on to paper or disk and retained for future reference. If you are asked in a year's time to arrange another conference, many of your thoughts and opinions about this occasion will be hazy or forgotten if you rely on your memory alone. Alternatively, you may be promoted or could leave the company, and your replacement might not know anything at all about conference management – so write a report! Make sure you include the following information:

Framework

It is sensible to set down all of the activities that you carried out when organizing, promoting and running the event – identifying the type of conference, recognizing goals, establishing a budget and so on. Specify their sequence and timings and add any comments and suggestions you might wish to make. For example, speakers must be booked *before* delegates are invited, so they can be used as an attraction. A venue and overnight accommodation need to be reserved well in advance to ensure the event is held where you want it to be. Sketch out some checklists as well, typically for choosing a venue, facilities, services and so forth.

Strengths

Do keep a record of what you did well – not so much to promote yourself (although there is nothing wrong with this!) but to ensure that due consideration is given to your winning approach and tactics next time. Perhaps a listing in a particular directory generated an excellent response, or a certain speaker was especially popular. When doing this though, you must be aware of *and* add a proviso – every conference is unique, and that directory, speaker, etc. may not be appropriate for another, different event later on.

Weaknesses

Just as important, you need to make a note of any mistakes that you made – perhaps you underestimated your budgetary requirements, misjudged the cash flow, had an indifferent theme which did not really appeal to delegates, used suppliers whose services were not up to standard, and so forth. Do identify the reasons why these mistakes occurred, which can almost certainly be attributed to inexperience. Suggest how these mistakes can be avoided next time around – include VAT and inflation in the budget, set aside a larger, initial sum to maintain cash flow, and so forth.

IMPROVING YOURSELF

Without doubt, you will have come a very long way since you were given the job of staging this event. To begin with, you probably had absolutely no knowledge at all whereas now you feel you could be employed as a professional conference organizer (almost!). However, there is more you can do to improve your performance in this field. In particular, you can read as much as possible about the subject, and attend training courses in various aspects of conference management.

Reading

It may be worthwhile subscribing to a trade magazine such as *Conference and Exhibition Fact Finder* in order to keep up to date with the developments in this industry. (See *Further Reading*, page 77.) Also, you may find it beneficial to read through as many books as possible on topics such as budgeting and cash flows, publicity and advertising and public speaking and presentations. Mastering these tasks and duties will help you to improve your conference management skills.

Training
Most trade bodies run a range of training courses for their members and other professionals operating in their field. The Association of Conference Executives (ACE) and the Meetings Industry Association (MIA) are particularly active in this area, setting up a host of seminars and training programmes regularly throughout the year. (Refer to *Useful Addresses*, page 79.)

PLANNING AHEAD
If this conference was regarded as successful and you remain in your current position, then it is likely that you will be handed the responsibility for staging another one in six, twelve, eighteen months time, or whenever. Thus, you may want to plan ahead for the future *now*, to ensure the next event is a success, not a failure.

Success
To be a success, you must work through the same, basic activities again – but this time, you should jiggle their order into a better, more logical sequence and adjust their timings too, so that everything is done at the right moment rather than being rushed. You must build on the winning approach and tactics that you identified, *if* they are relevant this time. Also, you should take steps to eliminate the mistakes you made first time around.

Failures
Failure! What failure? You have organized, promoted, run and evaluated one conference, identified its strengths

and weaknesses and know how to remedy them, *and* have improved yourself by reading and going on training courses. So how can it fail? You now possess all of the skills and expertise needed to be a winner – and to stage the perfect conference each and every time. Go for it!

CHECKLIST FOR SUCCESS – TEN

- Have you written a report about the conference?

- Did you make a note of all your activities, and your strengths and weaknesses on this occasion?

- Have you set about making improvements in any weak areas?

- Have you read magazines and books, and attended various training courses?

- Have you planned ahead for next time?

- Is the next conference going to be a success?

FURTHER READING

British Conference Destinations Directory published by the British Association of Conference Towns (BACT), First Floor, Elizabeth House, 22 Suffolk Street, Queensway, Birmingham B1 1LS; Tel: 021 616 1400; Fax: 021 616 1364.

A free of charge, annual guide to different conference destinations in Britain, from Clwyd through Leeds to Perthshire. Each destination entry includes a description of the area, details of conference facilities and a contact name and address plus telephone and fax numbers for further information.

Conference and Exhibition Fact Finder published by Batiste Publications Limited, Pembroke House, Campsbourne Road, Hornsey, London N8 7PE; Tel: 081 340 3291; Fax: 081 341 4840.

A monthly magazine, available on subscription at £27.00 per annum for United Kingdom subscribers (1994 rate, subject to change). It contains conference news, general features often on recent events and refurbished venues as well as a venue directory and a buyers' guide to conference facilities and services.

Conference Green and Blue Books published by Benn Business Information Services Limited, Riverbank House, Angel Lane, Tonbridge, Kent TN9 1SE; Tel: 0732 362666; Fax: 0732 367301.

It costs £63.00 (1994) for these two annual directories, regarded as the bibles of the conference industry. The *Green Book* details conference venues, unusual locations, unconventional features and so on, while the *Blue Book* sets out technical information regarding capacity, dimensions, lighting, power and so forth.

Conferences and Exhibitions Diary published by
Themetree Limited, Prebendal Court, Oxford Road,
Aylesbury, Buckinghamshire HP19 3EY; Tel: 0296
28585; Fax: 0296 436622.

A quarterly, loose–leaf publication printed in March,
June, September and December, and available on subscription at £45.00 per year (1994 rate). It lists conferences for the forthcoming year and also incorporates
useful data about organizers and services.

USEFUL ADDRESSES

Association of Conference Executives (ACE), ACE International, Riverside House, High Street, Huntingdon, Cambridgeshire PE18 6SG; Tel: 0480 457595; Fax: 0480 412863.

Established in 1971, ACE has a membership of more than 600 firms involved in organizing, marketing, accommodating and servicing conferences. Amongst the many benefits available to its members are a monthly newsletter, a what's on calendar of ACE and other trade bodies activities and various seminars and training courses offered at discount rates.

British Association of Conference Towns (BACT), First Floor, Elizabeth House, 22 Suffolk Street, Queensway, Birmingham B1 1LS; Tel: 021 616 1400; Fax: 021 616 1364.

This is a professional association representing over 100 conference destinations in the British Isles. It aims to support and co-ordinate the activities of its members by promoting their venues and facilities in the national and international marketplace. Of particular help to conference organizers. BACT will provide a complimentary directory on request and a free venue-finding service, and also stages an annual 'CONFER' exhibition in London where organizers can meet representatives of the different destinations.

British Tourist Authority (BTA), Thames Tower, Black's Road, Hammersmith, London W6 9EL; Tel: 081 846 9000; Fax: 081 563 0302.

The function of the BTA is to promote Britain to overseas visitors. Thus, businesses that are organizing conferences which may be of interest to foreign visitors can turn to the Authority for help with information and advice. In some situations, the BTA can also assist with the costs of staging events, typically sharing the expense of producing and distributing promotional literature.

Connect, 36 Collegiate Crescent, Sheffield, Yorkshire S10 2BP; Tel: 0742 683759; Fax: 0742 661203.

This is a consortium of nearly 100 college and university venues throughout the British Isles which offer conference and accommodation facilities for small and large events from rural to city-centre locations. Like the British Association of Conference Towns, it provides a complimentary venue-finding service for organizers, matching requirements with its members' venues.

Meetings Industry Association (MIA), 34 High Street, Broadway, Worcestershire WR12 7DT; Tel: 0386 858572; Fax: 0386 858986.

The MIA is the professional body for the meetings industry in the United Kingdom. Those firms which are members are involved in planning, managing and supplying services to the marketplace. The Association offers various benefits for its members including seminars and training programmes to help improve performance.

PERFECT BUSINESS WRITING

Peter Bartram

In every job, writing plays a part – and the ability to write well helps you to perform your job better. Good writing is important both for you and for your organization. It enables you to communicate effectively with your colleagues. It advances your career prospects. It contributes to the success of your company by improving communication with customers and suppliers – and it enhances the corporate image.

If you, like so many people, lack confidence in your writing ability, this book is the perfect answer.

£5.99 Net in the UK only.

ISBN 0-7126-5534-4

THE PERFECT BUSINESS PLAN

Ron Johnson

A really professional business plan is crucial to success. This book provides a planning framework and shows you how to complete it for your own business in 100 easy to follow stages.

Business planning will help you to make better decisions today, taking into account as many of the relevant factors as possible. A carefully prepared business plan is essential to the people who will put money into the business, to those who will lend it money, and above all to the people who carry out its day to day management.

£5.99 Net in UK only.

ISBN 0-7126-5524-7

THE PERFECT NEGOTIATION

Gavin Kennedy

The ability to negotiate effectively is a vital skill required in business and everyday situations.

Whether you are negotiating over a business deal, a pay
rise, a difference of opinion between manager and staff,
or the price of a new house or car, this invaluable book,
written by one of Europe's leading experts in negotia-
tion, will help you to get a better deal every time, and
avoid costly mistakes.

£5.99 Net in UK only.

ISBN 0-7126-5465-8

THE PERFECT PRESENTATION

Andrew Leigh and Michael Maynard

When everything seems to go right, you perform at your absolute best, your audience reacts enthusiastically and comes away inspired, then you've given the perfect presentation!

But success is underpinned by hard work, and the authors of this book provide the necessary framework on which to base your presentations, under the headings of the 'Five Ps': Preparation, Purpose, Presence, Passion and Personality.

Many major organizations have used material from the courses on which this book is based. Now you can gain those benefits – at a fraction of the cost.

£5.99 Net in UK only.

ISBN 0–7126–5536–0

THE PERFECT APPRAISAL

Howard Hudson

Implementing the right appraisal scheme can significantly improve employee and company performance.

Most companies have some form of appraisal scheme in place, yet they get very little out of it. A properly conducted appraisal scheme can raise performance standards, cut costs and in some cases 'revolutionize' the business. This concise and invaluable handbook provides managers and organizations with a practical blueprint for appraisal, and shows how they can obtain maximum benefit from appraisal schemes.

£5.99 Net in UK only
ISBN 0-7126-5541-7

THE PERFECT DISMISSAL

John McManus

Dismissals are wretched occasions for everybody concerned; but unhappiness and unpleasantness can be kept to an absolute minimum by the use of this book.

It tells both employer and employee how to avoid legal pitfalls and their associated costs. Just as importantly, it emphasizes human considerations – common sense, fairness and the dignity of the individual.

The Perfect Dismissal provides a clear and well-balanced summary of a complex subject.

£5.99 Net in UK only.

ISBN 0-7126-5641-3